W9-AYQ-957

What in the World Is a Guitar?

Mary Elizabeth Salzmann

Consulting Editor, Diane Craig, M.A./Reading Specialist

A Division of ABDO

ABDO
Publishing Company

visit us at www.abdopublishing.com

Published by ABDO Publishing Company, a division of ABDO, P.O. Box 398166, Minneapolis, Minnesota 55439. Copyright © 2012 by Abdo Consulting Group, Inc. International copyrights reserved in all countries. No part of this book may be reproduced in any form without written permission from the publisher. Super SandCastle™ is a trademark and logo of ABDO Publishing Company.

Printed in the United States of America, North Mankato, Minnesota
092011
012012

 PRINTED ON RECYCLED PAPER

Editor: Elissa Mann
Content Developer: Nancy Tuminelly
Cover and Interior Design: Colleen Dolphin, Mighty Media, Inc.
Interior Production: Aaron DeYoe
Photo Credits: Shutterstock, Thinkstock

Library of Congress Cataloging-in-Publication Data

Salzmann, Mary Elizabeth, 1968-

What in the world is a guitar? / Mary Elizabeth Salzmann.

p. cm. -- (Musical instruments)

ISBN 978-1-61783-206-2

1. Guitar--Juvenile literature. I. Title.

ML1015.G9S26 2012

787.87'19--dc23   7712

2011023168

Super SandCastle™ books are created by a team of professional educators, reading specialists, and content developers around five essential components—phonemic awareness, phonics, vocabulary, text comprehension, and fluency—to assist young readers as they develop reading skills and strategies and increase their general knowledge. All books are written, reviewed, and leveled for guided reading, early reading intervention, and Accelerated Reader® programs for use in shared, guided, and independent reading and writing activities to support a balanced approach to literacy instruction.

Contents

What Is a

A guitar is a musical instrument.

Guitar?

body

bridge

The main parts of a guitar are the tuning pegs, the neck, the fingerboard, the frets, the strings, the body, and the bridge. Most guitars have six strings. But there are guitars with 12 or even 18 strings!

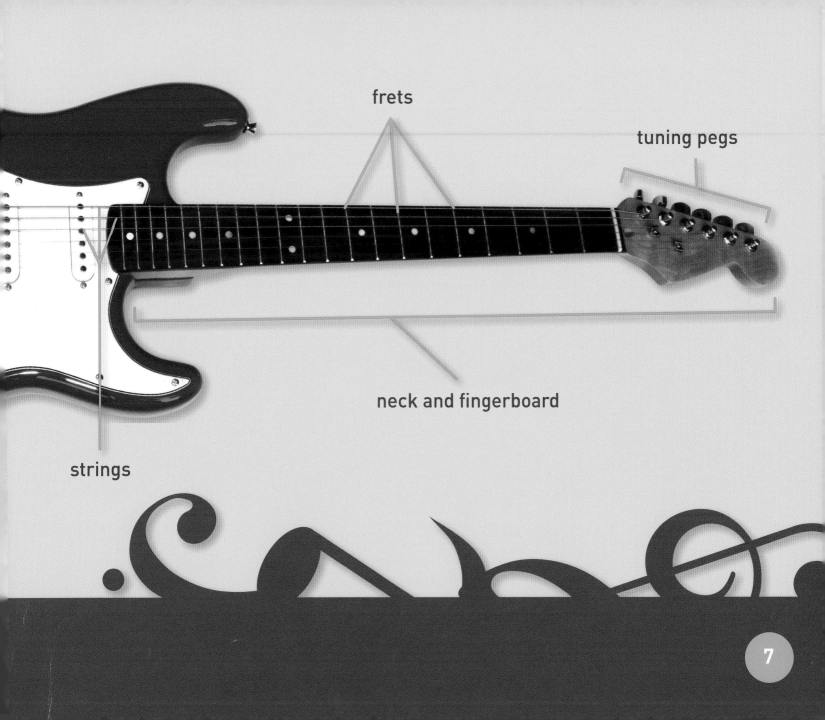

frets

tuning pegs

neck and fingerboard

strings

An **acoustic** guitar is **hollow**. It has a hole under the strings.

An electric guitar is **solid**. It **plugs** into an **amplifier**.

To play the guitar, the guitar player **strums** or **plucks** the strings. A guitar can be strummed with the fingers or a guitar pick.

The guitar player presses the strings against the fingerboard to play different notes.

Let's Play

the Guitar!

Sean got an electric guitar for his birthday. He wants to start a rock band with his friends.

Maria's mom is teaching her how to play the guitar. She shows Maria how to play different notes.

Kevin is playing an **acoustic** guitar. His guitar teacher is playing an electric guitar.

Samantha practices a song on the guitar. She likes to play the guitar and sing.

Find the Guitar

a.

b.

c.

d.

a. violin

b. guitar (correct)

c. clarinet

d. drum

Guitar Quiz

1. All guitars have six strings. True or False?

2. An **acoustic** guitar is **solid**. True or False?

3. A guitar can be played with the fingers or a guitar pick. True or False?

4. Maria is learning the guitar from her mother. True or False?

5. Kevin is playing an electric guitar. True or False?

ANSWERS: 1. false 2. false 3. true 4. true 5. false

Glossary

acoustic – not needing an amplifier to make music. Acoustic is pronounced *uh-KOO-stik*.

amplifier – something that makes sound louder.

hollow – having an empty space inside.

pluck – to pull an instrument's strings with one's fingers.

plug – to stick the end of a cord into an outlet or other hole.

solid – having no space inside. Not hollow.

strum – to brush the fingertips over the strings of an instrument, such as a guitar.